Maths Activities

Caroline Matusiak

This bo

Bright Ideas
FOR Early Years

Published by Scholastic Ltd,
Villiers House, Clarendon Avenue,
Leamington Spa,
Warwickshire CV52 5PR

© 1990 Scholastic Ltd
Reprinted 1992, 1993, 1995

Written by Caroline Matusiak
Edited by Juliet Gladston
Sub-edited by Jackie Cunningham-Craig
Designed by Sue Limb
Illustrations by Lesley Smith
Photographs by:
Caroline Matusiak pages 5, 9, 35, 63,
67, 75 and 81
Bob Bray page 19
Cover by Martyn Chillmaid

Artwork by Liz Preece,
Castle Graphics, Kenilworth
Printed in Great Britain by
The Alden Press Ltd, Oxford

British Library Cataloguing in Publication Data
Matusiak, Caroline
  Bright ideas for early years.
  Maths activities.
  1. Nursery schools. Teaching
  I. Title
  372.1102

  ISBN 0-590-76387-3

Contents

Introduction 5

Everyday maths 9
Silhouettes 11
Picture labels 12
Signs 13
Treasure chests 13
Photograph books 14
Clocks and watches 15
Day and date 15
Ourselves 16
Height chart 16
Comparing ourselves 17
Handprints 18
Portraits 18

Everyway maths 19
Story 22
Reading stories 22
Storyboard 23
Puppets 24
Soft toys 25
Rhymes 26
Paint 27
Paper shapes 27
Printing with bricks 28
Tessellating with shape 28
Moving shape 29
Butterfly prints 29
Painting pictures 30
The writing centre 31
Making books 31
Wrapping presents 32
Making badges 32
The computer 33
Computer toys 34

Natural materials 35
Dry sand 36
Filling and emptying 36
A spoonful 37
Bottled up 37

Sandwheel   38
Colander and sieve   38
Wet sand   39
Sand pies   39
How big?   40
Heavy or light?   41
Sand combs   41
Making an impression   42
Sand patterns   42
Water   43
Full and empty   43
Pouring tea   44
Bottles   44
One litre   45
Float or sink?   46
Boats   47
Blowing bubbles   47
Bubbles   48
Making a splash   48
Ripples   49
Snow   49
Clay and dough   50
Sharing   50
What shape?   50
Making cakes   51
Patterns   52

Construction   53
Wooden bricks   55
Silhouettes of bricks   55
Building with bricks   56
Exploring shape   56
Moving shape   57
Looking at shape   57
Making plans   58
Tracks and roadways   59
Making maps   60
Scrap materials   61
Practical maths   61
Sorting materials   62
Making shapes   62

Junk modelling   63
Sticking shapes   64
Making clothes   65
Woodwork   66

Role play   67
Ordering by size   69
Shape   69
Time   70
Clock   70
Money   71
Mail order   71
Setting up shop   72
Paying with money   72
Visits   73
Making equipment   73

Outdoor and physical play   75
Large construction   76
Climbing frames   77
Toys with wheels   77
Moving   78
Body shapes   78
Ring games   79
Educational visits   80

Food   81
Spreading   82
Non-standard measures   83
Standard measures   84
Baking   84
Cooking   85
Cutting apples   85
Fruit and vegetables   86
Popping corn   87
Growing cress   88
Shopping list   89
Shopping   89
Paying for goods   90

Records   91
Book list   94
Resources   94
Photocopiable page   96

For Tony, Tom and Rose

Introduction

Activity, experience and language in context are the focus of maths in the early years. For example, children learn about shape as they build with bricks and junk; sort and match while tidying up; become familiar with number names as they sing rhymes; learn about the function of money as they shop and the purpose of measurement as they participate in making curtains for the home corner.

Adults, alert to the areas of mathematical learning, make the most of the potential offered by children's play and daily life. Listening to and talking with children about what they are doing puts their experience into words which can be recalled in different situations.

Opportunities to develop children's mathematical language and understanding can arise in their physical, social and imaginative play. Adults should recognise every opportunity to enhance children's awareness of maths, be it the shape of a pocket or the length of shadows on a sunny day.

Life skill

Maths underlies many of our daily activities and household tasks, whether we are shopping, cooking, knitting, filling the car with petrol, or putting up shelves. To complete these tasks requires planning, estimating, predicting outcomes, measuring and a knowledge of number, shape, money and time. Maths is not just something 'done at school', and before we try to help children, it is paramount that we recognise maths as a life skill, rather than an intellectual exercise. Try listing the various ways you use maths in daily life.

Attitudes

Many people have a dread of maths. Care needs to be taken that we do not transmit any negative feelings we may have about maths. This can be done unconsciously through overheard comments, such as, 'I can't add up to save my life'. We need to be clear about our own feelings towards maths and if necessary, overcome personal prejudices.

Attitudes are also acquired from peers and family. Peer groups often follow the example that we set. We must therefore ensure that we demand the same participation and standard of commitment to mathematical activities from girls as well as boys. It is important that we expect and encourage girls to participate fully in building and making, perhaps initially by developing a home corner activity such as making a food processor. Boys need to be equally encouraged to play in the home corner — fathers coming in to feed babies can help to break down traditional role models.

To begin to break down negative attitudes from home, 'I couldn't do maths when I was at school', requires an active parent information and participation programme.

Individuals

Children enter playgroups, nurseries and reception classes with different experiences, abilities and interests. The skilled teacher of young children is sensitive to these and interacts with the child as an individual, taking into account her level of development. We need to observe what children are doing before we intervene, offering the appropriate vocabulary. Children may well start talking about what they are doing or thinking as we approach. It is important that we listen to what children say and interact accordingly. On the other hand, imposing ideas on children who may not have already acquired the necessary experience and concepts to understand what is required, can equally cause them to become disenchanted.

Involving parents

Parents usually want to know about their child's learning environment and progress. They may also want to know how they can complement their child's learning at home and contribute to school life.

To help involve parents:
- Foster a relationship with parents founded on mutual trust and respect.
- Provide parent information booklets and displays about learning.
- Prepare guidelines on how to complement this learning at home.
- Make parents aware of the many maths activities that they can share with their child at home such as sorting washing, matching pairs of socks etc.
- Provide clear record sheets (see photocopiable page 96) so that parents can observe the development of their own child and share this with you.
- Offer suggestions for parental involvement including baking, using computers, educational visits and table games. Informed parents are in a better position to develop the maths potential of these activities.
- Inform parents of current topics and projects so that they can contribute items of interest to the class collection and involve their child in similar investigations at home.
- Start a toy home loan scheme. Include jigsaws and table games to encourage matching for shape and colour. These can be obtained from jumble sales and older children.

Display

Maths needs to feature in classroom displays. This can be achieved in a number of ways:
- When writing captions for display, focus on the maths learning that underpins children's work, for example,

the problem-solving in model making.
- In the discovery centre develop the maths potential of topics, for example, chart the height of seedlings as they grow, perhaps by drawing a line or cutting string to the same length.
- Have a maths activity display, for example on shape, identifying, handling, matching two- and three-dimensional shapes, or asking 'Can you fit these shapes together?'.
- Involve children from the start with the sorting and matching activities needed to gather material together for display.
- Let the children sort the relevant objects for the display table. This gives a greater sense of ownership and enables them to associate ideas presented on the display table with the world around them. The display table becomes a record of sorting activities, a source of information, as well as a stimulus to further investigation.

About this book

This book offers ideas for structuring an environment where mathematical activity is purposeful, relevant and meaningful. Activities present a wide range of experience. Children are encouraged to plan and carry out their own activities, concentrating on tasks, solving problems, discussing ideas and working together. Above all, they should enjoy it.

The mathematical objective of all areas is emphasised, with particular reference to:

● Number: including opportunity to match one-to-one, use number names, count, estimate and make patterns.

● Shape and space: including experiencing shape in a variety of situations, opportunity to build with a variety of shapes.

● Measures: including weight, height, time, money and capacity. Opportunity to compare without measuring, and use non-standard and standard measures.

● Handling data: including observing and naming attributes, and sorting objects.

'Objectives' are not intended to be achieved by using isolated activities but should be met as part of everyday classroom life. Planning to make a flan in the food area would encompass many of the suggested activities, for example, estimating how much is needed, shopping, carrying the weight of items and paying with money, baking, using non-standard measures and talking about the duration of time before it is cooked, as well as fractions in dividing the flan between the children.

'What you need' indicates resources that are available for use. These resources are used in many different ways and the activity focuses on one of these.

'What to do' gives ideas for supporting and extending children's play when the appropriate opportunity arises. These are suggestions to adapt and use according to the needs and interests of your children. They are intended to open out new possibilities rather than restrict the use of equipment.

'Talk about' is an important part of early mathematical learning, putting into words what children are doing, seeing and handling. It offers suggestions for introducing relevant vocabulary. However, take into account the individual interest of each child, and other mathematical opportunities which may arise as a result of this activity.

'Follow-up' gives further ideas and suggestions for expanding the initial activity.

Everyday maths

Chapter one

Maths for the young child should not be seen as an activity isolated from everyday life. Children need plenty of first-hand experience before they are asked to work with second-hand ideas. Therefore, adults need to be aware of the mathematical potential of daily activities, and to use them as a base for learning: fastening coat buttons, matching one button to one hole; mixing paint with one brush per pot. It is important that children are encouraged to participate fully in all aspects of classroom life, including preparation and tidying away. Putting newspapers over a table top in preparation for sticking activities, provides invaluable experience in covering an area. The final product may well not be as neat as an adult's polished and practised article, but this must be set against the learning potential for young children.

Real jobs

We should actively consider what children can be encouraged to do for themselves. When children see the necessity of knowledge about number, time, money and even fractions, they become motivated to learn more about it and to improve their skills.

The importance of children participating in real jobs cannot be over emphasised. When new curtains are needed for the home corner or a bike needs repairing, it is better that this is completed with the children. They watch as the adult works, asking questions and participating at their own level. This offers a model of applied maths, demonstrating the necessity of measurement and accuracy. Children become familiar with terms of measurement and ascertain how to use rulers, tape measures and other tools.

Provision

Children's learning depends on decisions concerning provision and organisation so you need to take into account the mathematical potential of equipment that you offer to children. If only random bottles are offered in water play, children will not be able to experience the need to fill a litre bottle twice with half litre bottles and four times or more with smaller bottles.

This potential for learning about capacity and related sizes can be realised with carefully chosen graded equipment.

The role of the teacher

● To plan: carefully structure an environment where mathematical activity is purposeful, relevant and meaningful. The provision of equipment must take into account mathematical learning so that during free play each area offers the potential for each child to develop ideas. In our interaction with the children, we need to be aware of mathematical potential as children play.

● To model: make explicit, mathematical activities that you are engaged in during the day. Too often these are not brought to the children's attention. Putting up displays shows children the application of maths as you estimate and cover areas. Talk as you work, offering children the chance to participate. The result may not appear as tidy, but children really feel the display belongs to them, particularly if they have had the opportunity to decide which work should be displayed and to choose colour mounts and backgrounds.

● To initiate: initiate mathematical activities which children can pursue. Sorting the pile of wellington boots by the door into matching pairs is a popular activity.

● Topics: in a carefully considered environment, children will naturally involve themselves in mathematical activities, but this can be extended and enhanced by introducing and purposefully developing children's interests.

Silhouettes

Spade

Objective
Shape and space: matching three-dimensional objects with two-dimensional shapes.

What you need
Classroom objects including sand and water equipment, coloured paper, transparent sticky-back plastic, scissors, pencil.

What to do
Look at the object to select the most appropriate angle. Consider its particular features. On the reverse of the paper, draw round the object.

Cut out the silhouette and cover it in sticky-back plastic, leaving an edge of 3cm. This can now be replaced on its original backing paper until you are ready to mount it.

Make silhouettes with the children, talking about the attributes of objects,

whether they have curves or corners, handles or holes.

Children enjoy choosing objects and making their own silhouettes.

NB Cut out all the silhouettes for one panel before starting to mount them. This enables you to position them efficiently. At first use Blu-tack to mount silhouettes so that they can be re-arranged if necessary. Stick-on plastic hooks allow equipment to be hung on flat surfaces. (Do not use sharp outward facing hooks.) Silhouettes can be placed on walls, screens and shelves.

Talk about
Does it match? What does it look like?

Follow-up
• Try silhouetting three sizes of equipment, for example, funnels and jugs to encourage matching for size.
• Use paper the same colour as the object, to encourage matching for colour.
• Try silhouetting the equipment from one area in one colour, for example, water equipment in blue, to encourage matching for shape and to ensure the return of equipment.

Picture labels

Objective
Handling data: sorting to specific criteria using picture labels.

What you need
Supplier's catalogue, scissors and transparent sticky-back plastic.

What to do
Many construction materials, for example LEGO, have a variety of pieces, not all of which will be depicted on the label. Children learn which ones belong together through familiarity with the materials.

Select a picture of the equipment from the catalogue. Cut this out and cover it with sticky-back plastic, leaving at least 2cm at the edge so that it will adhere to the container or shelf. Use the picture labels in:
• The writing centre where pictures of scissors, pencils and crayons can be displayed on the outside of containers.
• Scrap materials where photographs of materials stored together can be displayed on their respective containers. NB Ensure that pictures and photographs show both girls and boys involved in the activity.

Talk about
Is it the same? Where does it belong?

Signs

Objectives
Number: counting figures and associating them with the relevant numeral.

What you need
Paper, pencil, scissors, number stencil, figure stencil and transparent sticky-back plastic.

What to do
Decide how many children can play safely and effectively in each area of the room. Using the stencils, draw round the appropriate numeral and the corresponding number of figures. Cut these out and stick them on to paper. Cover this with sticky-back plastic leaving an edge of 2cm for easy mounting. Repeat this for each area.

Talk about
How many? Number names, less than, not more than.

It also encourages them to count each other and to apply their maths.

Treasure chests

Objectives
Number: sorting and matching using 'lost bits'.

What you need
The 'lost bits' drawer or boxes of buttons, shells or oddments.

What to do
Tidying up 'lost bits' fascinates children as they try to determine their original area or activity. Boxes of buttons, shells and other items are viewed as treasure chests by children who sort and match using their own criteria. It is useful to discuss why certain objects have been put together. Offer suggestions for sorting; for example, the round, blue buttons.

Talk about
Do they belong together? A set.

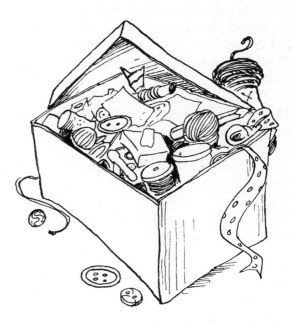

Photograph books

Objective
Measures: understanding time by using photographs of a sequence of events.

What you need
A camera, paper and adhesive.

What to do
Take photos of the daily routine: children arriving, activity time and group time. Stick these in time sequence order in a book. Print captions for the photos.

Talk about
What time is it?

Children enjoy looking at photos of themselves involved in familiar activities. Discuss what is happening in the photo and ask what will happen next.

Follow-up
• A set of these photos can be stuck on to separate cards for children to sequence.

• Ask parents for photos of children's daily routine – getting up, having breakfast and going to school. Make a book and a set of sequencing cards from these. These give an opportunity to talk about morning, afternoon and evening.

• Take photos of the school and outside play area in different seasons to create a focus for talking about winter, spring, summer and autumn.

• Read story books that depict a sequence of events, for example, *Maisie Middleton* by Nita Sowter (Fontana Picture Lion) and *Moonlight* by Jan Ormerod (Picture Puffin).

Clocks and watches

Objective
Measures: using clocks and watches to measure time.

What you need
Clock and watch.

What to do
Refer to the clock or watch at intervals. Try to link clock time with an event known to the children: 'It's 12 o'clock and time for lunch'.

Talk about
Clock time, in half an hour.

Day and date

Objectives
Measures: providing familiarity with the days of the week and months of the year.

What you need
A day, date, month and weather board. These are available commercially or can be made using card and felt-tipped pens.

What to do
Change the weather board daily with the children. To give children a reference point try to link each day with an activity, 'Today is Wednesday and we go into the hall for movement'. The weather gives an opportunity to talk about the past, 'Yesterday, it was raining, but today it is sunny'. It also gives a chance to discuss the month, season and associated weather.

Talk about
Days of the week, date, month, season and associated weather.

15

Ourselves

The maths potential of this topic includes measuring, number and shape. Role play can feature a clinic which provides a meaningful context for the height chart suggested below. A mirror provides experience of three-dimensional into two-dimensional and also reflection.

Height chart

Objectives
Measures: comparing and measuring for size using handprints and becoming familiar with the length of a metre.

What you need
A long strip of paper, painted handprints, a metre rule and sticky labels.

What to do
Cut out the handprints and mount these in a row. Next to this, mount either the metre rule or a drawing of it.

Stand each child in turn against the chart and mark their height with a named sticky label. Count how many hands high. The span, the width between the thumb and little finger, was an early form of measurement. Refer to the metre rule. It is difficult for children to relate to centimetres but with increasing experience they can understand more than a metre or less than a metre.

Talk about
How tall? Taller than, not as tall as, shorter than.

Comparing ourselves

Objectives
Number: sorting and making sets using the children themselves.

What to do
● Make the children aware of colour, pattern and height. Ask the children to group themselves according to whether they are, for example, 'wearing red', 'wearing stripes' or are 'taller than Emma'.
● Ask three or four children to stand together. This time let the children guess what they have in common. Give clues if necessary.
● This can be developed further by using two or more categories — wearing red stripes; taller than Emma but smaller than Lee.
NB Categories need to be chosen sensitively so that all the children feel part of a group and equally valued. The emphasis should be on the 'same' not 'different'.

Talk about
What sort of? Taller than, smaller than, the same.

Handprints

Objective
Shape and space: looking at three-dimensional and two-dimensional shapes using the body.

What you need
Thick fingerpaint, paper and a bowl of soapy water to wash hands.

What to do
Cover the palm of the hand with paint and print on to paper. Turn the hand and print with the other side. These are useful for making the wallchart (see page 16).

Talk about
What shape? How many? How big?

Follow-up
• Try making footprints using talcum powder and dark paper. Fix the print to the paper with hairspray. The children will need help with this activity.
• Ask the children to consider the number, size and shape of toes and compare them with the print.

Portraits

Objectives
Number: matching and counting by asking the children to look at themselves.

What you need
Paper, paintbrushes, an unbreakable mirror and a large variety of ready-mixed paint or powder paint.

What to do
Ask the children to look closely at themselves in the mirror and to describe their hair and eye colour. Let them choose or mix the appropriate colour when painting themselves. Count and name the facial features together, for example, eyes, lips and eyebrows. Consider the length of hair and colour of clothes. Choose or mix colours to match. NB If ready-mixed paint is used, it is important that colours represent the hair, eye and skin colour of all the children.

Talk about
What colour? How many?

Everyway maths

Chapter two

Children develop physical, social and intellectual skills simultaneously. A child using large bricks learns about tessellation, the way shapes fit together, practising the hand control needed to balance bricks, while talking and planning with a friend.

Children acquire many different mathematical concepts from one activity. Many possibilities for development and interaction open up as they play. Listen to children's explanations of what they are doing and know the child's stage of development before intervening.

It is important to consider the following factors.

- First-hand experience: The starting point for all maths is first-hand experience. Children need plenty of experience with a variety of materials in a context, before they are ready to understand the idea of measuring weight, identifying shape and using number.
- Success and motivation: Young children need to be presented with tasks and materials with which they will be successful. Children who are looking for challenges, can be presented with tasks that are open-ended, leaving scope for individual decisions and interpretation.
- Investigation: As children play, they explore, experiment and assimilate ideas. The greater the variety of experiences involved in an activity, the more potential there is for learning. The child's goal provides the impetus for doing and learning.
- Concentration and perseverance: Children need to be allowed, as far as possible, to continue their task until it is completed. Children cope with set-backs and possible failure more readily when the tasks are self-initiated. Intervene before real frustration sets in.
- Planning: Planning involves children thinking ahead and working with ideas. It means that they need to predict outcomes, and organise materials to achieve their aim. However, plans should provide a framework for learning and not be a strait-jacket, preventing children from exploring unforeseen possibilities that arise during play.
- Working together: Playing together presents a particular challenge to young children who have to learn the social skills and language facility necessary to build relationships with others. It is only gradually that children develop common goals and work together to accomplish them.
- Physical co-ordination: A balanced programme of physical activity is

required to ensure that children develop the fine motor control necessary to manipulate equipment successfully and efficiently.

Equipment should present a variety of challenges, both in the diversity of their function and in the nature of physical skills demanded by their use. This builds up the experience and manual dexterity required for the practical application of maths.

● Intellectual skills: Children need to develop the following intellectual skills:

Communication — Mathematical ideas associated with position, shape and number arise throughout the classroom. Be aware of these and be prepared to introduce them at the appropriate time and place.

Children talking with you or their peers as they work, helps to formulate ideas and develop important vocabulary. It is of vital importance to listen to what children say about what they are doing, rather than make assumptions which may be erroneous.

Children need a lot of experience to give meaning to words they hear and may even use in the correct way, enhancing their vocabulary and enriching their command of language and ideas.

Representation — In maths, as in writing, figures or symbols stand for numbers and their operations, such as adding or subtracting. Initially they need to develop their own symbols.

Encourage imaginative and symbolic play throughout the classroom, as this lays the foundation for accepting and manipulating the abstract figures of later maths.

Problem-solving — Children need encouragement to tackle problems for themselves. Problem-solving entails having the confidence to try, the motivation to succeed and willingness to think of alternatives, if success is not forthcoming. It is this ability to concentrate and persevere that needs to be nurtured. Children often learn more through careful consideration of things that have not worked out than those that do. For this reason, all work that children have undertaken should be valued.

Reasoning — Solving problems in a stimulating and rich environment encourages children to explore and ask questions. This often occasions play to be repeated, to see if it happens again and minor modifications may well be included to test and examine influential factors. The important aspect is that the child is starting to reason and is becoming aware of repeated patterns which then begin to influence future expectations.

Story

Many stories provide a rich source of mathematical language. It is important that maths is seen as part of imaginative activities as well as more practical ones.

Reading stories

Objective
Developing mathematical language through reading stories.

What you need
A selection of children's stories.

What to do
The joy of story is that children appreciate maths ideas in a meaningful imaginative context. Story captures a child's emotions and interest.

Don't break off a story to emphasise a maths idea. Intervention should serve only to enrich a child's understanding.

Do browse through before or after reading the story, discussing events, characters and maths ideas in a meaningful way.

Suggestions for story:

Titch by Pat Hutchins (Picture Puffin), which features three children of different ages.

There's No Such Thing as a Dragon by Jack Kent (Blackie), which is about a tiny friendly dragon that grows bigger.

The Very Hungry Caterpillar by Eric Carle (Picture Puffin), where counting and naming days of the week are an integral part of the story.

1 Hunter by Pat Hutchins (Picture Puffin). This counting book presents number in an amusing manner.

Storyboard

Objective
Developing mathematical language through using a storyboard.

What you need
A large board covered in felt, different coloured felt or fabric, scissors, adhesive, needle and thread.

What to do
Cut out felt characters from children's favourite stories. Tell the story using the felt characters introducing the relevant maths ideas. Leave the storyboard and figures in the book corner for the children to retell the story using the mathematical language.

Many folk tales offer scope for developing mathematical language:

'The Three Billy Goats Gruff' offers relative size and counting.

'Goldilocks and the Three Bears' offers relative size, counting, and one-to-one correspondence, that is one bowl for each bear etc.

'The Three Pigs' offers cardinal numbers, one, two and three, as well as ordinal numbers, first, second and third.

Puppets

Objective
Developing mathematical language through using puppets.

What you need
A selection of puppets either commercially-bought or hand-made. They can be made in a variety of ways using spoons, cardboard inner tubes or paper bags for a body.

What to do
Using one or more puppets and perhaps some easy props, tell a story that features mathematical language in some way. Work the puppet to perform the actions as the words are introduced. Leave the puppet in the book corner for children to retell the story using the puppet to relate the words to actions.

Follow-up
● Move a puppet around a colourful box with a lid. Introduce language of position such as, on top, inside, behind, at the side of, between and underneath.
● Take a puppet for a ride on a toy car. Introduce language of direction and speed, such as, backwards, forwards, slowly and quickly.
● Using a puppet, a washing line, coloured pegs and sets of dolls' clothes, introduce counting, naming colours, matching colours and making patterns with the pegs. Use the dolls' clothes for matching pairs, for example, socks, gloves, shoes and matching sets, such as clothes for warm weather, bedtimes and rainy days.

Soft toys

Objective
Developing mathematical language through using soft toys.

What you need
Soft toys of different sizes, colours and fabric, such as fur, fabric with different patterns — striped, spotted, checked and plain. Try jumble sales or older children who have outgrown these toys and may be willing to donate them.

What to do
Introduce these toys to the children one at a time. Look at their features and describe them, for example, two ears, whiskers, four legs and made from grey fur. Choose a name that is based on one of its features, for example, Furry.

Look at features they have in common, for example, four legs. Count how many have four legs. Count how many are blue. How many have spots?

Make families, such as the Whisker family.

Look at ways in which they are different, for example, different colours, sizes, shapes and fabric.

These soft toys can be used for stories that will develop other mathematical language (see 'Puppets' on page 24).

Talk about
How are they the same? How are they different? Compare them for size, colour and features.

Rhymes

Objective
Learning mathematical language through rhymes.

What to do
Finger and action rhymes are an enjoyable way of learning number names and counting. Many introduce the idea of the empty set or none, when fingers or children are counted.
Try these rhymes:
● Five currant buns in a baker's shop.
Small and round with sugar on the top,
Along came a boy/girl with some money one day,
Bought a currant bun and took it away.
● 1 2 3 4 5 once I caught a fish alive, 6 7 8 9 10 then I let it go again.
Why did you let it go?
Because it bit my finger, so.
Which finger did it bite?
This little finger on my right.
● Here is a beehive, where are the bees? (Fold hands together.)
Hiding away where nobody sees. (Look inside folded hands.)
See them come creeping out of their hive. (Raise five fingers one at a time.)
1 2 3 4 5 zzzzzzzzzzzzz. (Wave fingers to represent the bees flying.)
Rhymes can also introduce position:
● Hickory Dickory Dock, the mouse ran *up* the clock.
The clock struck one, the mouse ran *down*.
Hickory Dickory Dock. (Wiggle a finger as a mouse and let it run up and down your arm.)

● *Up* a tall candlestick crept little mousie brown. (One arm upright for the candle and walk a finger, the mouse, from the other hand up the arm.)
Right to the top and he couldn't get *down*.
He called for his grandma, 'Grandma',
But his grandma was in town,
So he curled himself into a ball and rolled himself right *down*. (Curl the finger and roll it down your arm.)
These and other suitable rhymes can be found in *This Little Puffin* by E Matterson (Penguin).

Paint

Paint gives the opportunity for children to represent. Painting pictures encourages children to observe the shapes of things around them. It also encourages the naming, sorting and mixing of colours. Patterns can be made with a brush or by printing with objects.

Paper shapes

Objective
Measures: covering an area by painting on different shaped paper.

What you need
Paper of different shapes — square, oval, circle, semicircle, triangle and rectangle etc.

What to do
Give these shapes to the children to paint or print on. At first, the children will paint over the edges of unusual shapes, like triangles, until they learn to accommodate the shape. This is evident at the stage when they cover the entire sheet in paint. As the children become accustomed to these shapes, their printing and painting shows an increasing response to the shape. They start to paint and print inside the shape.

Talk about
What shape? Shape names, cover.

Follow-up
- Try paper of different sizes.
- Explore many different triangles and rectangles.
- Try Polo shape paper.

Printing with bricks

Objective
Shape and space: three-dimensional into two-dimensional by printing with bricks.

What you need
Paint, bricks of different shapes including cuboid, cylinder and cube.

What to do
Print with each face of the brick. Cylindrical bricks can be rolled and either end used for printing.
  Printing with bricks gives an opportunity to consider the faces of a solid shape.

Talk about
What shape? How many faces? Three-dimensional and two-dimensional shape names.

Follow-up
Try printing with spheres, for example, marbles and roll-on deodorant bottles filled with paint.

Tessellating with shape

Objective
Shape and space: tessellating by printing shapes together.

What you need
Paint, bricks and other objects, for example, plastic cartons and packaging.

What to do
Print rows of a shape trying to join them together. Try this using a variety of shapes, regular and irregular.

Talk about
Do they fit together? Straight sides, curved sides.

Moving shape

Objective
Shape and space: movement along a line by printing the same shape.

What you need
Paint, bricks and other objects including packaging.

What to do
Choose one shape. Make a print and then move it along and repeat this shape. After a while, move the shape along (translation) and this time turn it (rotation) and then print.

Talk about
What shape? Which way? The same way, upside down.

Follow-up
When the children are familiar with printing, encourage them to make patterns. Make a pattern for them to copy or start a pattern for them to continue.

Butterfly prints

Objective
Shape and space: symmetry where both sides of a shape are identical.

What you need
Paint of different colours and paper.

What to do
Fold a piece of paper in half. Paint on one side of the paper. Press both sides together to produce a mirror image.

Talk about
What pattern? The same.

Painting pictures

Objective
Shape and space: identifying shapes in children's paintings.

What you need
Paints of different colours and paper.

What to do
Look together at shapes of houses, flats, windows and other familiar objects. As the children paint pictures, observe how shape is used to represent objects. See how many different shapes they have used and how they are combined.

It is important to listen to their explanation for choosing to paint a 'house' using that shape, rather than to impose ideas.

Talk about
What shape?

The writing centre

Although not immediately associated with maths, a writing centre where children have the opportunity to make their own books, posters and labels encourages estimating, measuring and counting. Number and letter shapes may well be written together, as a child imitates print seen in the environment.

Ideas

- Make sure there are numbers as well as words available in the writing area.
- Order forms and receipt books encourage children to write numbers.
- Have numbers and letters displayed at child height in this area.

Making books

Objective
Problem-solving.

What you need
Paper, mark-making equipment such as pens, pencils and chalks, as well as a hole punch, stapler, wool, string, sticky tape, scissors, paper-clips, plastic binders and tags.

What to do
Making books encourages children to plan and carry out a practical maths activity, involving problem-solving, measuring and estimating.

Cut or tear paper to make regular or irregular shapes. Join these together to make books. Try punching holes and then sewing with thread. Wind sticky tape around one end of the thread to make a 'needle'.

Talk about
How? What else could we try?

Follow-up
Try making these types of books:
- concertina,
- fan,
- different shapes, for example, triangle and circle.

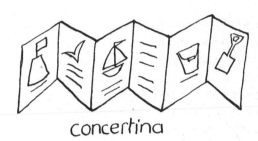

concertina

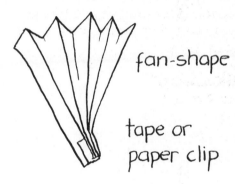

fan-shape

tape or paper clip

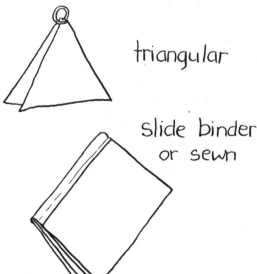

triangular

slide binder or sewn

rectangular

Wrapping presents

Objective
Measures: covering a three-dimensional shape by wrapping presents.

What you need
Large sheets or rolls of paper, for example, wallpaper, old greetings cards, felt-tipped pens and pencils.

What to do
Wrapping up presents involves estimating, measuring and problem-solving.

Make 'presents' in the scrap materials area. Bring these to the writing area to be wrapped and labelled. Cut labels of different shapes and sizes from greetings cards. Felt-tipped pens and pencils encourage the children to write their own messages.

Talk about
How much? How many? Is it enough? Covers, does not cover.

Making badges

Objective
Number: writing children's ages.

What you need
Coloured sticky-back paper, scissors and felt-tipped pens.

What to do
Cut 'badges' of different shapes, for example, circles, stars and diamonds. Ask the children to choose one, or cut their own. Write on each child's age. Many children will want to write on their own name and age.

Talk about
How old? What number?

Follow-up
Make a birthday card for a friend. Write on it the age of the child. Write the number in letters and figures either on the card or for the child to copy.

The computer

Computers offer an introduction to technology and the modern method of handling data. Young children take readily to the computer and many have access to one at home.

Before using a program with young children, ask yourself:

• Does it take into account hand control and different abilities by allowing the child to decide when the programe moves forward? A 'beat the clock session' proves very frustrating for young children trying to fulfil the demands of the screen and those of the keyboard.

• Is it an open-ended program with an emphasis on language development, problem-solving and investigation?

• Does it encourage the children to talk and work together?

• Can children of all abilities use it, with each child contributing and benefiting in her own way?

• Is it a program designed to 'teach' number or shape? Is the emphasis on 'getting it right'? Such programs usually involve sorting and matching the appropriate shape or number. This can be a useful form of consolidating previous knowledge for children who can already do this, but can prove confusing for those who cannot.

• Is the screen print large and clear?

• Are children sufficiently familiar with computer graphics to enable them to identify them and complete the program?

Computer toys

Objectives
Shape and space: exploring direction and movement.

What you need
A computer toy and rechargeable batteries.

What to do
This popular activity encourages children to use mathematical language as they plan and program the path of the toy robot or vehicle.

Encourage the children to program this for themselves and discover what it can do. It is possible to program a series of commands that determine the direction and distance that the toy robot will travel. This gives rise to estimating, predicting and problem-solving.

• Set simple targets for the toy to reach, for example, the table.

• Make these targets more difficult, for example, around the chair and under the table to the door.

• Make easy to understand charts using the symbols and design of the keys on the class computer toy. State or draw a starting point, include a program sequence and ask, 'Where are you now?' The children can draw or write the answer.

Talk about
How far? What direction? Forwards, backwards, turn, turn to the left or right, straight ahead.

Natural materials

Chapter three

Water, clay, dry and wet sand should be available all the time for children to explore and experiment with. It should be remembered that the handling of these materials can have a therapeutic effect on children: clay and sand can never be broken and may be used to channel aggression; water and dry sand are soothing to touch and can have a calming effect. You know your children and should be aware of times when emotional demands supersede all others.

   The possibilities for learning mathematical concepts are infinite and not confined to any one material. The divisions which follow take account of the properties of the materials. The flowing of dry sand and water lends itself to concepts of speed and time, but that does not imply that playing with wet sand precludes this learning, for example, taking a long time to push a car slowly through heavy wet sand.

Dry sand

Children develop mathematical concepts as they learn about the properties of sand. They discover that dry sand runs downwards and through holes; it takes the shape of the container and finds its own level. Grains of dry sand can be poured, sieved and easily transferred from one container to another.

This gives ample opportunity to develop concepts of time, speed and capacity.

Sand trays are available for inside use, but outside sand-pits, large enough for children to sit and play in, offer scope for exploration on a larger scale. Visits to a beach provide this with the added bonus of seaweeds, stones of different sizes and colours, as well as shells.

Filling and emptying

Objective
Measures: comparing capacity by filling and emptying containers with sand.

What you need
Dry sand, containers of different shapes and sizes, including a bucket, plastic cup, yoghurt pot.

What to do
Fill a container, and empty it into another. A small container can be emptied into a large, and vice versa. Compare amounts and levels, noticing when the receiving container is full or empty. Transparent containers allow the children to decide when it is nearly full or nearly empty.

Talk about
How much? Full, empty, more than, less than, same amount.

36

Bottled up

Objective
Measures: comparing time and speed by watching sand flow.

What you need
Dry sand, one transparent plastic bottle with one hole pierced underneath and one with six or more holes underneath.

What to do
Ask the children to fill the two bottles with sand and then to hold them up and watch the sand flow out. Compare the levels of sand in both bottles as they empty. Also ask the children to compare the length of time it takes for them to empty.

Talk about
How long? Slowly, quickly, faster than, slower than.

A spoonful

Objective
Number: estimating capacity using different-sized spoons and sand.

What you need
Dry sand, a small container, a variety of spoons, for example, a teaspoon, a tablespoon, a ladle, a mustard spoon.

What to do
Estimate how many teaspoonfuls it takes to fill the container. Fill the container counting the spoonfuls. Try again using a bigger spoon.

Talk about
How much does it hold? Teaspoonful, tablespoonful, ladleful. How many? Names of numbers.
  Encourage the children to use and refer to everyday measures.

Sandwheel

Objective
Measures: comparing time and speed by using a sandwheel.

What you need
Dry sand, a sandwheel and containers.

What to do
Pour a large amount of sand over the wheel. Then let sand trickle slowly over the wheel. Watch how quickly the wheel turns. Compare this with the flow of sand.

Talk about
How quickly? Slowly, slows down, faster, spins, turns.
   Discuss how quickly the wheel turns.

Colander and sieve

Objective
Measures: comparing time and speed by watching the flow of sand.

What you need
Dry sand, utensils with holes such as colanders, sieves, flowerpots, a perforated spoon, a flour shaker, a funnel, netting of different gauges, such as that used for fruit packaging.

What to do
Show the children how to cup their hands and fill them with sand. Ask them to open their fingers and watch as the sand flows between their fingers and falls into the sand pit. Try again. This time ask them to open their fingers a little at a time.
   Fill other equipment with sand. Watch as the sand finds a path through every hole. Predict how quickly the sand will flow out of equipment with large holes and with one small hole.

Talk about
How quickly? Slowly, fast, how long? A long time, not so long.

Wet sand

Wet sand can be moulded and shaped; patterns and impressions can be made in it. Children love to shape and mould sand using their hands. They enjoy patting, squeezing, stroking and slicing sand with the edge of their hand or finger. In this way, it gives children the opportunity to discover the mathematical concepts of space, shape, size and pattern. Water added to sand shows how it becomes very runny and heavy as patterns and moulds disappear. Children need to see for themselves how much water is actually added and how the sand slowly changes in consistency. At times, it makes for useful comparisons if wet and dry sand are in the same tray.

Sand pies

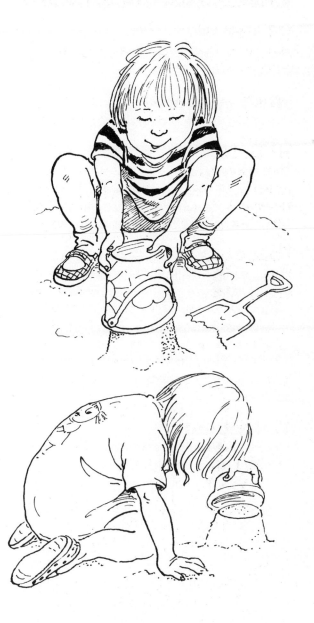

Objectives
Shape and space: filling and making three-dimensional shapes with wet sand.

What you need
Wet sand, moulds, bucket, bowl, egg cup, plastic trowel and brick moulds, packaging such as yoghurt pots, margarine tubs, ice-cream cartons etc. Choose containers with both flat and curved surfaces, in regular and irregular shapes.

What to do
Fill containers with sand and make pies. Making a sand pie is an achievement in itself for very young children and they should practise this until they can fill and pack a container successfully. Children are proud of their first sand pies and may wish to make one in a place where it can be saved and shown to their parents. Sets of brick moulds and trowels enable children to fill and make cuboid shapes.

Place brick shapes next to each other to make walls.

Talk about
What sort of surface? Flat, level, curved, fits together.

How big?

Objectives
Measures: comparing size and ordering by size using sand pies.

What you need
Wet sand, graded containers or stacking beakers.

What to do
Make sand pies using different size beakers. Afterwards, choose the same size beaker to fit back over each sand pie.

Arrange beakers in order of size, starting either with the smallest or the largest. Make a sequence of similar sand pies.

Ask the children if they can make a sand pie tower, stacking sand pies on top of each other, starting with the largest. This encourages estimation and problem-solving.

Talk about
How big? Small, large, larger than, smaller than, same size.

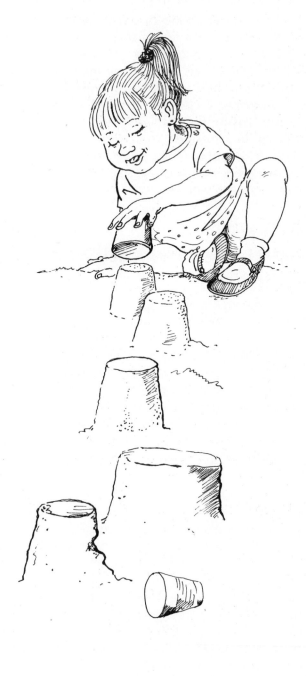

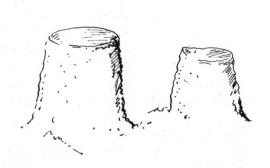

Heavy or light?

Objectives
Measures: comparing and carrying weights, and using the balance scales.

What you need
Wet sand, balance with two removable buckets, spade.

What to do
Fill one bucket with wet sand and leave the other one empty. Hold one bucket in each hand. Children need to feel the difference for themselves in order to understand the idea of light and heavy, which precedes measurement of weight. Put the containers on the balance. Ask how we can make them balance.

Talk about
How heavy is it? Light, heavy, same weight, heavier than.

Sand combs

Objective
Shape and space: learning about direction by pulling objects through sand.

What you need
Wet sand, rake, sand combs, fork.

What to do
Encourage the children to pull their fingers over the sand, opening and closing them. Then pull sand combs, a rake and a fork across the sand. As the fork travels straight across the sand, it makes parallel lines. Interesting curves are made as the fork is pulled round corners.

Try making it in a circle or a wavy line.

Talk about
Which way do the lines go? Straight across, upwards, downwards, in a curve.

Making an impression

Objective
Shape and space: looking at different faces of an object by making impressions in wet sand.

What you need
Wet sand, shells, cotton reels, pine cones, boxes, balls.

What to do
Start by making handprints with both the front and the back of the hand. Compare the impressions left in the sand. Use different faces of each object to make impressions, discussing each one as it is made. Cylinders, cuboids and pyramids offer a variety of shapes.

Talk about
What shape? Circle, triangle, square, rectangle.

Sand patterns

Objective
Number: making patterns in sand.

What you need
Dry or wet sand, shells, twigs, pine cones, beads.

What to do
Using small objects, encourage the children to make their own patterns. You can also start a pattern for the children to continue or repeat, giving a choice of objects and design.

Talk about
Which one? The last one, the next one. The first, second etc.

Water

Water runs downwards taking the shape of its container and finding its own level — add food colouring so that water levels in transparent containers are easily visible. This gives opportunties for learning about capacity and displacement. Water also offers some interesting moving patterns. The daily use of liquids for drinks, washing themselves, washing equipment and watering plants involves the children in estimating the amount of water required and the kind of container most suitable for a particular activity.

Ornate toiletries provide a range of random containers. Hollow handles and other appendages are interesting for children to fill and watch as the water level rises.

A water tray with a ledge on which to place equipment while pouring is a good idea. For those trays without ledges, a Formica plank across the tray provides a stand for bottles. Experiment with different water levels and temperatures.

NB Many of the activities suggested for dry sand (see pages 36–38) are also applicable to water.

Full and empty

Objective
Measures: introducing capacity and other everyday terms of measure.

What you need
Jugs and a variety of containers.

What to do
Pour water into a container. Sometimes it will be full, at other times it will reach different levels.

(see pages 36–38)

Talk about
How much? Empty, full, to the brim, overflowing, half-full, half-empty, nearly full, cupful, jugful.

Pouring tea

Objective
Measures: introducing capacity by pouring a fixed amount of liquid into different containers.

What you need
Water, teapot, mugs and cups of different capacities.

What to do
Pour water from the teapot to see how many cups can be filled. Choose one cup and estimate how many cupfuls it takes to fill the teapot. This can be repeated with different size cups.

Talk about
How many cupfuls? The same number, more than, less than.

Bottles

Objective
Measures: looking at capacity by filling smaller bottles from a fixed amount of liquid.

What you need
Graded plastic bottles based on one litre, for example, a litre, 0.5 litre, 0.25 litre.

What to do
Ask the children to estimate how many bottles the litre bottle will fill. Fill the litre bottle with water and pour this into the 0.5 litre bottles. Refill the bottle and use 0.25 litre bottles.

Talk about
How much? Twice as much, half as much. Introduce the terms 'a litre' and 'half a litre' as the children become familiar with its capacity.

One litre

Objective
Measures: showing how containers of different shapes can have the same capacity.

What you need
Water, containers of the same capacity, for example one litre, but different shapes, including a plastic bottle, a cylinder, a cuboid, a shallow tray, commercial packaging with irregular shapes.

What to do
Pour water from one container to another, watching how the same amount of water takes the shape of its container. Confirm this by pouring the water back into the original container.

Young children need a lot of experience pouring water from one container to another before they can do it accurately without spilling any.

Introduce the funnel as a way of transferring water into narrow-necked bottles.

Talk about
How much? Same amount, takes the shape, to the top, fill.

Float or sink?

Objective
Handling data: sorting to a specific criterion.

What you need
Water, a variety of natural and man-made materials such as wood, plastic, cork, shells and nails. Two trays, preferably with picture labels indicating floating and sinking.

What to do
Ask the children to place the objects in the water and to decide whether they float or sink. Place each article on the appropriate tray.

Talk about
Is it floating? Is it sinking? On the surface, underneath the water, on the bottom.

Follow-up
The properties of water give the children the opportunity to sort objects according to attributes that are not readily observable. Try sorting for the following:
- materials that absorb water;
- materials that are waterproof;
- substances that dissolve in water.

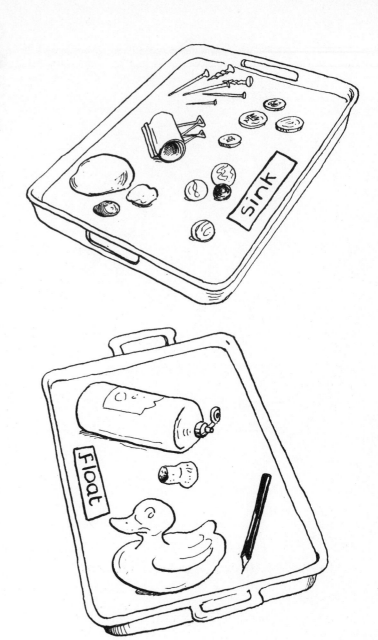

Blowing bubbles

Objective
Shape and space: looking at spheres, circles and arches.

What you need
Strongly coloured water with bubble liquid added, bubble blowers of different sizes, white paper.

What to do
Blow bubbles. Observe the shape and size. When bubbles float down, look at the wet ring left behind. Use the paper to catch a bubble and see the ring more clearly. This can provide a souvenir of favourite bubbles as well as offering scope for comparison. Rainbows on bubbles and those appearing around the water tray on a sunny day present some colourful arch shapes.

Talk about
What shape? Sphere, ring, circle, arch.

Boats

Objective
Shape and space: making shapes on water.

What you need
Water, a stick, a boat.

What to do
Draw a finger over the surface of the water to make a V-shaped wash. Try this using a stick and then a boat.

Talk about
What sort of shape? V-shape, surface, gets wider.

Bubbles

Objective
Measures: looking at capacity by filling containers with bubbles.

What you need
A transparent container, a small amount of water and bubble liquid, a straw.

What to do
Blow through the straw into the bubble liquid until the frothy mixture reaches the top.

Talk about
How much? Not very much, to the top, overflowing, full of bubbles.

Making a splash

Objective
Shape and space: making shapes on the surface of water.

What you need
Water, stones, food colouring.

What to do
Drop small stones from various heights on to the water. Watch the patterns made. Try using drops of food colouring.

Talk about
What sort of a shape? Ring, gets wider, small.

Ripples

Objective
Number: making patterns on the surface of water.

What you need
Water, a drinking straw.

What to do
Move a hand through the water, making waves. Blow on the water surface using the straw to make ripples. Compare the still surface with a rough one.

Talk about
What sort of pattern? Ripples, waves, higher.

Snow

Objective
Shape and space: making shapes with snow.

What you need
A water tray filled with snow.

What to do
The children can mould and shape snow. Leave containers of snow to melt. Watch how the shapes change and how far up the container the resulting water reaches.

Talk about
What shape? Change shape, a round snowball, a flat snow pie.

Clay and dough

At the early stages, children enjoy using these materials for their own sake, exploring their potential. They offer a material where shape can be changed, starting flat and then rolled into 'sausages' or balls, but the original quantity remains constant. This involves shape, size, number and conservation of quantity.

Children build their own regular and irregular shapes. Biscuit shape cutters can be used with dough, but ensure that children do not come to depend on them for all their shape-making. Cutters do give children the chance to make and consider regular shapes, but it is important for them to build up their own shapes, thus becoming aware of the curves and flat surfaces which make up three-dimensional shapes.

With dough, different shapes can easily be combined to form others. More dough can be added to make a larger shape, or some taken away to make a smaller one. With clay, on the other hand, children can work from a lump, gently smoothing it into a form. Clay can also take thumping and slapping as children work out individual frustration.

Sharing

Objective
Number: estimating and dividing.

What you need
Dough.

What to do
This is a job that is often done by an adult, but it provides an opportunity for the practical application of maths.

Place the dough on the table and ask a child to divide it into two, or as many portions as there are children intending to use it. Comparisons of amount ('He's got more than me!') ensure that the quantities are equal.

Talk about
How much? Some each, share, divide into two, same amount each, estimate.

What shape?

Objectives
Shape and space: looking at the different faces of a solid shape.

What you need
Dough, bricks of different shapes including pyramids and cuboids.

What to do
Press the bricks into the dough. Press each side of the brick into the dough and compare the shapes that are made.

Talk about
What shape? Three-dimensional shape names and two-dimensional shape names, for example, sphere and circle.

Making cakes

Objective
Number: one-to-one correspondence as a prelude to counting.

What you need
Dough, bun tin, bun cases or a plastic egg box.

What to do
Encourage the children to use the dough to make 'cakes' for the tin, placing one in each section. They may wish to decorate each 'cake' with a 'cherry'.

Talk about
How many? One each, one in each case, one on top of each cake.

Patterns

Objective
Number: making patterns with everyday objects.

What you need
Dough, surfaces with raised patterns such as potato masher, open-weave fabrics, plastic packaging.

What to do
Press the surfaces into the dough to make patterns. Originally this idea came from the children who were busily leaning forward to press their knitted jumpers on the dough!

Talk about
What sort of pattern? Is it the same? Does it repeat?

Construction

Chapter four

Construction activities, where children design and make their own models, give opportunities for the practical application of mathematics. While building, they are making three-dimensional shapes, considering size, sorting the necessary pieces and estimating the number required. As children become more adept, symmetry and tessellation of shape becomes evident. Models may include the use of levers, wheels and other moving parts.

A variety of construction materials enables children to become acquainted with the properties and potential of a wide range of equipment. Use commercially produced large and small construction equipment, as well as scrap materials, usually packaging collected by parents.

The following are some ideas for what you need for successful small construction.

- Equipment that is versatile and open-ended. Equipment which is defined in its use limits children's play and adults' expectation.
- Construction equipment that consists of a variety of shapes which can be successfully combined in an infinite number of ways, requiring children to use their imagination.
- Equipment that includes a variety of pieces which may suggest a general use, such as a window or opening, but which can be put in buildings, vehicles and other designs of the child's own making.
- Construction equipment that takes account of the physical control of all children.
- Sufficient equipment for children to build without encountering the frustration that a lack of adequate key pieces presents.
- Levers, axles, wheels and other moving parts, as children will best learn how to use them if they are presented as part of construction sets.
- Wooden or plastic people and animals to give children a purpose for building small houses and enclosures. They encourage children to build layouts on a similar scale when working together, and stimulate imaginative play when the model is finished.
- A range of equipment that presents alternative methods of attachment.
- Several construction areas that offer different equipment, with a close pile carpet or table, enabling models to balance.

Wooden bricks

Wooden bricks, which are available in many shapes, can be fitted together to demonstrate mathematical relationships, for example, semicircles that combine to form circles. Many of the following activities arise naturally as children use bricks.

Silhouettes of bricks

Objective
Shape and space: matching three-dimensional bricks with their two-dimensional silhouettes.

What you need
A set of size-related wooden bricks, open shelves, coloured paper, transparent self-adhesive plastic, scissors, pencils, felt-tipped pens.

What to do
Place bricks on the shelves in a way that demonstrates mathematical relationships; for example, two half-size bricks alongside a full-size one.

On the reverse of the coloured paper, draw around the bricks. Cut out the shape. Use the felt-tipped pen to draw in any divisions between the bricks. Cover with transparent self-adhesive plastic, leaving 2cm around the edge. Stick on to the shelf.

Talk about
What shape? Do they match? Shape names.

Building with bricks

Objective
Shape and space: looking at structures that children build with bricks.

What you need
Building bricks.

What to do
Look at the structures that children build with bricks.
- What shapes have been chosen?
- How are these shapes combined?
- Is there an attempt at pattern or symmetry?
- Are the children exploring the vertical and balance in making a 'tower'.
- Are they exploring the horizontal and tessellation, for example, in making a 'floor'.

Talk about
What shape? Pattern, balance.

Exploring shape

Objective
Shape and space: building with three-dimensional shapes.

What you need
A set of size-related wooden bricks, wooden or plastic figures, vehicles and animals, wooden planks.

What to do
Let the children explore the shapes and their attributes; for example, the curves on cylinders and the angles on cuboids. Introduce the planks. Use these as slopes. Place the different faces of bricks on the slope, such as a cylinder.

Talk with the children as they start to combine shapes, finding out shapes that fit together and structures that balance. Figures, vehicles and animals will encourage the children to make models such as a bus or a house.

Talk about
What shape? The face, curved, flat, roll, balance, fit together.

Looking at shape

Objective
Shape and space: looking at shape from different angles and perspectives.

What you need
A set of wooden bricks.

What to do
Ask the children to select several bricks of the same shape. Encourage them to move and turn the shapes, looking at them from above, underneath, the side and at an angle. Look at them close to and at a distance.

Talk about
Which way? On top of, upside down, underneath, the side, same, different.

Moving shape

Objective
Shape and space: movement along a line.

What you need
A set of size-related wooden bricks.

What to do
Ask a child to choose several bricks of one shape. Then encourage her to move one brick without turning it (translation), and to move and turn a brick (rotation). Try this with regular shapes, such as cubes and cuboids, as well as with irregular shapes. Bricks can also be placed against each other like a mirror image (reflection).

Talk about
Which way? Turn, same way, upside down.

Making plans

Objective
Shape and space: three-dimensional into two-dimensional shapes by drawing plans of children's models.

What you need
Construction equipment like wooden bricks, interlocking bricks or scrap materials, clipboard, paper and pencil.

What to do
Draw a plan of a child's model. Ask the child what features are to be included. Using an apprenticeship approach, let the child add more features.

Leave a clipboard in the construction area and encourage the children to draw plans or 'pictures' of their favourite models. Display the plan and model together.

Talk about
What shape? How many?

Although the final plan may not always resemble the model to an adult's eye, the accompanying discussion reveals the child's appreciation of the shape in relation to each component and to the whole.

Tracks and roadways

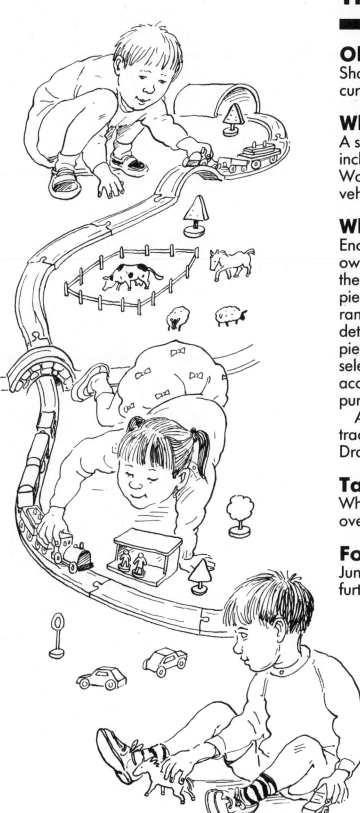

Objective
Shape and space: combining straight and curved tracks.

What you need
A set of roadway or railway tracks including straight and curved sections. Wooden or plastic figures, animals and vehicles.

What to do
Encourage the children to make their own tracks and roadways. In doing this they are seeing how straight and curved pieces combine. Early tracks may well be random constructions where the shape is determined by access to the nearest piece. With experience, the children select a curved or straight track according to whether or not it suits their purpose.

At this stage, ask the children to plan a track with you, and then try to make it. Draw the plan on paper for reference.

Talk about
What shape? Which direction? Under, over, round a corner, straight, curved.

Follow-up
Junctions, tunnels and bridges provide further scope for combining linear tracks.

Making maps

Objectives
Shape and space: introducing scale, looking at objects from different viewpoints and three-dimensional into two-dimensional shapes by making maps.

What you need
Pictorial playmats, travel brochures, road or railway tracks, large sheets of paper, clipboard, paper and pencil.

What to do
Introduce pictorial playmats with tracks for cars and trains. Look with the children at travel brochures, featuring overhead views of the locality.

Encourage the children to plan and make their own track. A child's view while putting tracks together is from above. When the track is finished, ask the children to look closely at it, discussing its shape. Ask them to draw a map or 'picture' of it. Features that are important to the child may well be exaggerated. At first, the children draw the track without considering the 'look' of the track on paper.

To introduce scale, start with large paper and gradually introduce smaller sheets.

Talk about
What shape? Which direction? From above, overhead.

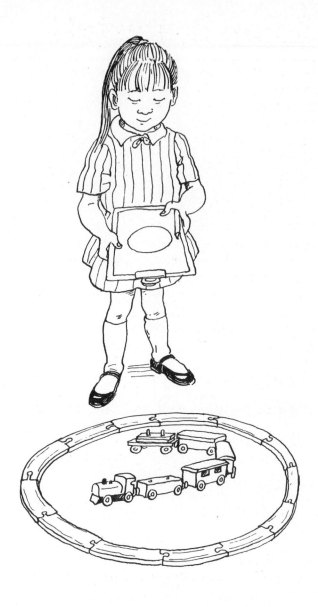

Scrap materials

The use of scrap materials for making models and collages of children's own design gives rise to problem-solving with materials of different properties. This places more demands on children's own imagination and planning. Indeed, these materials can be cut, sawn, bent or torn to achieve their goals. First of all, children explore their attributes: those that are flexible and those that are rigid. They discover different ways of fastening materials together with adhesive, paste, sticky tape, paper-clips and paper-fasteners, or by sewing. They try to attach curved surfaces to flat ones, and in doing so they discover those shapes that fit together.

Practical maths

Objective
The practical application of maths skills.

What you need
Scrap materials and a variety of fastenings.

What to do
Encourage the children to design and make their own models. This involves:
- Problem-solving as the children fasten shapes and materials together.
- Estimating how much or how many.
- Measuring using non-standard units.
- Investigating the possibilities of shape and size.
- Predicting possible outcomes.
- Representing as they use their imagination to create models.

   As the children are making their models, look for:
- Sorting for size, shape and colour.
- One-to-one correspondence, such as matching one bottle top to each

compartment of an egg box.
- Pattern and symmetry.

Sorting materials

Objective
Handling data: sorting scrap materials to specific criteria.

What you need
An open shelf, a trolley, plastic boxes, paper, felt-tipped pens, transparent self-adhesive plastic.

What to do
Get the children to sort the scrap materials into the containers. Choose categories according to the attributes of materials; for example, thread, which could include wool, string, ribbon, pipe-cleaners and shredded paper. Encourage parents to keep a container by their kitchen bin to collect items useful for school. The children can sort these into the relevant boxes.

Talk about
Do they belong? Which box? The same as.

Making shapes

Objectives
Shape and space: making a three-dimensional shape and considering its two-dimensional net.

What you need
Boxes of different sizes and shapes, like cereal, chocolate, toothpaste, soap, cake and biscuit boxes.

What to do
Open out and flatten boxes of different sizes and shapes. When the children make their models they can reconstruct these boxes. Re-assemble the boxes inside out to make it easier to paint them.

Talk about
What shape? Face, corner, angle.

Junk modelling

Objective
Shape and space: building with three-dimensional regular and irregular shapes.

What you need
A variety of scrap materials, for example, boxes, cartons, cardboard tubes, paper, card, paste, PVA adhesive, sticky tape, paper-clips, stapler.

What to do
Encourage the children to make junk models, designing their own models and choosing the appropriate materials. In this way they discover shapes that fit together. They can combine different shapes in a variety of ways.

Ask the children whether they can make a model that moves or a boat that floats as they become more adept at selecting and combining materials.

Talk about
What shape? Shape names, fit together, join.

Sticking shapes

Objective
Shape and space: combining two-dimensional shapes to make pictures and patterns.

What you need
Coloured paper cut into shapes, for example, squares, triangles, polygons, stars, semicircles and others. Plain paper, scissors and paste.

What to do
• Make a collage using a variety of shapes. Discover shapes that fit together, turn shapes and move shapes.
• Make patterns and pictures using these shapes.
• Cut paper in different shapes, for example, circles and triangles. Ask the children to choose a sheet. This can be covered with smaller coloured shapes. Let the children choose from a variety of small shapes or cut their own. Older children can try to cover the sheet without overlapping and without leaving any gaps.

Talk about
What shape? Two-dimensional shape names.
NB Technically speaking paper shapes have three dimensions.

Follow-up
Try making pictures and patterns using:
• commercial plastic and wooden shapes;
• tiles or different shapes that fix on to a board. These are useful for younger children who can easily knock free-standing shapes out of place; they are also commercially available.

Making clothes

Objective
Measures: estimating and measuring to fit.

What you need
Scrap materials including fabric, milk bottle tops, paper, thread, needle, string or ribbon, masking tape, tape measure.

What to do
Let the children make clothes for toys, themselves or each other. Hats, belts, skirts, cloaks and aprons can be made using large lengths of fabric, such as old curtains.

Estimate how much material is needed, and choose a fabric length. Demonstrate accurate measuring by putting the material in place and marking it, or by using string or ribbon. Introduce a tape measure and demonstrate its use.

Join edges with masking tape and sew others.

The end product is worn with pride by the child, although it may not appeal to adult eyes.

Talk about
How long and how wide? Measure, fit, the right size, too long, too wide.

Follow-up
Try making jewellery — crowns, necklaces, bracelets, ear-rings — using thread, silver paper and pictures from greetings cards.

Woodwork

Objectives
To use and become skilled in the use of many different tools, and to learn to select the most suitable tool for the job.

What you need
Woodwork bench with clamp. Small-sized adult tools including hammers, pliers, hacksaw, screwdriver, bradawl, sand paper, nails and screws of various sizes, wood offcuts.

What to do
Ask the children to explore making durable models. The shape, size or texture of the wood may suggest models to them. They will otherwise need to estimate and cut wood to suit their purposes. At first, they will enjoy building up skills in sawing and using hammers; only later will they want to combine materials to make models. This area provides all the scope for maths present in the scrap materials, as many of those materials are similarly used by children in the woodwork area, namely cork and foil.

Talk about
Which tool? What does it do? Tool names.

Role play

Chapter five

The home corner is the focus of children's role play. Consider carefully the mathematical potential of this area and provide the appropriate equipment for encouraging children to imitate, and demonstrate the weighing, measuring and sorting activities which are part of everyday life.

Resource boxes

It is possible to overload the home corner, and its size and the storage arrangements need to be taken into account to avoid this occurring. It may be advisable, where only a small space is available, to have a permanent stock of basic utensils, with resource boxes of supplementary equipment on hand, which can be introduced as required.

Role play area

As the children play in the role play area, they are:
• Sorting things that are suitable for their imagined setting.
• Estimating number or size.
• Matching one object to another or to one person.
• Using number operations such as adding and subtracting, in a very practical way.
• Using shape and space as furniture is re-shuffled to fit the same space, and pans are up-ended in the cupboard in an attempt to make them fit the space available.

Real jobs

Children enjoy participating in real jobs. Here are some suggestions:
• Decorating the home area with wallpaper. This involves estimating, measuring and covering an area. The children can design and print their own wallpaper using their hands, leaves or other items. This gives experience of shape and pattern.
• Making curtains and covers involves estimating, measuring with accuracy and covering an area. Patterns can be drawn on using special washproof crayons that are available commercially.
• Painting or washing furniture involves covering an area.

Ordering by size

Objectives
Shape and space: matching for and ordering by size.

What you need
Three sizes of pans with fitting lids and cooker rings to match. Three sizes of dolls with fitting clothes and three sizes of cots with fitting covers.

What to do
Three sizes of equipment encourage the children to match for size and to order by size. It also encourages comparisons of size. As the children match each pan with a lid and cooker ring, and dress dolls and put them to bed, they match for size.

Silhouettes of pans on shelves encourage matching for size at tidy-up time.

Talk about
How big? Big, middle size, little, smaller than, bigger than.

Shape

Objectives
Shape and space: looking at shape, parts of the whole shape and covering an area.

What you need
Large cloths of different shapes such as circle, triangle, oval, square and rectangle. Choose material with colours and patterns that emphasise their shape. Old curtains are useful.

What to do
Ask the children to use the material to cover areas of different shapes, such as the table, the window or the bed. They can decide which shapes are suitable to wear as cloaks or shawls. These cloths can also be used for 'picnics' which the children and toys can sit on. Ask how many children and toys fit on the different-shaped cloths.

At tidy-up time, discuss the different shapes that are formed as the material is folded and put away. Compare the circular cloth with a square one.

Talk about
What shape? How many sides? Cover the table, fold, fold in half, curve.

Time

Objective
Talking about time sequence through role play.

What you need
Books depicting the daily routine to encourage discussion and role play.

What to do
Invite the children to act out roles from the books or from their own experience. They will organise and arrange their actions into sequences, for example, go shopping, empty the bag, make dinner and serve it. You can say, 'First you made a cup of tea, and then we sat together to drink it. What shall we do next?'

Through role play children consider and re-enact many daily sequences from getting up to going to bed. This helps them to organise time into familiar daily routines, and prepares the way for introducing more difficult concepts which refer to the order of days, such as 'yesterday', 'last night', 'the next day' and 'tomorrow'.

Talk about
When? First, next, then, meals associated with different times, such as dinner time, tea time.

Clock

Objectives
Understanding the function of clocks and becoming familiar with clock times through role play.

What you need
A clock with moving hands and large numbers.

What to do
A clock encourages children to refer to time as part their role play. 'It's tenty clock and time for tea', is a typical example from a child who realises the reliance of adults on clocks to measure the passing day, but cannot yet read the clockface for himself. 'Bed time' for dolls and other children is accompanied by much pointing at the clock and finger-wagging. A child explains, 'Well, just one more story and then go to sleep'.

Talk about
What time is it? Clock times, such as ten o'clock, morning, afternoon, evening.

Money

Objective
Understanding the function of money and different ways of payment.

What you need
Items relevant to everyday finance including purses, home-made cheque books and bank cards, allowance books and money.

What to do
Real money can be polished and varnished to make it easily identifiable. This gives children the opportunity to become accustomed to the sight and weight of money. However, this may not be practicable for a number of reasons and realistic plastic money is an appropriate substitute.

Talk about
How much? Coin names, change.

Mail order

Objective
Role-playing a financial transaction.

What you need
Mail order catalogues, clipboard, paper, pencil.

What to do
Invite parents who organise mail order purchasing to talk with the children, bringing in samples and spare order forms. Cosmetic catalogues are popular.

Organise your own mail order catalogue by cutting out pictures of samples and sticking these on a sales sheet or in a book. The children can write a number indicating how many they wish to buy. Cash or 'cheques' can be exchanged.

Talk about
How much does it cost? How many? Cash, cheque.

Setting up shop

Objective
Role-playing a financial transaction.

What you need
A strong till, receipts, old used till rolls, money, home-made cheque books and bank cards. Shopping bags and cardboard boxes give an opportunity to see how many things fit in a certain space, and whether these can be re-arranged to include more.

What to do
Try setting up these shops:
• A toyshop with boxes from birthday or Christmas toys, soft toys and class equipment.
• A takeaway with packaging donated by the local store — make menu cards with prices.
• A supermarket, with packaging from everyday products. Trolleys and wire baskets are available commercially.
• A post office with stamps, either old used ones or home-made, envelopes of different sizes can be sorted into different size slots, shoe boxes can be used to make these. Sheets of paper and string to wrap parcels. Stationery and birthday cards for sale.

Talk about
How much? Coin names, cheque, receipt, change.

Paying with money

Objectives
Sorting, matching and counting coins.

What you need
Coins, card, transparent self-adhesive plastic.

What to do
• Make price labels for goods using sorting and matching; for example, by sticking different coins on the label so that the children have to search in the purse and match the ones needed.
• Make price labels sticking about three of the same coins on the card for the children to sort and count.

Talk about
How much? How many? Coin names.

Young children cannot understand that a five pence coin is worth five individual penny coins. They see the five pence coin as a single unit. However, they do become familiar with the names of coins, for example, ten pence, fifty pence and a pound, although to them these names do not carry any indication of their worth.

Visits

Objectives
Measures: buying and measuring and learning the phrases and procedures associated with them through role play and visits.

What to do
Before setting up a specific role play area such as a post office or shoe shop, organise a visit to the local branch. Do this with small groups of children if there is one within walking distance of the school. Buy goods that are needed for the class, perhaps stamps, and weigh a parcel or have someone fitted for shoes to demonstrate the use of the equipment and expertise.

Talk about
How much? Names of measuring equipment such as scales, foot gauge.

Follow-up
Try setting up the following:
● A shoe shop with a foot gauge, various sizes of shoes and boxes for ordering and comparing size. Footprint measure to match for size.
● A clinic with bathroom scales and height chart for the children to measure themselves and each other.

Making equipment

Objectives
Practical application of maths skills through making equipment.

What you need
Large cardboard boxes, paint, adhesive and scrap materials.

What to do
Use the large boxes to make 'houses' or 'buses'. Smaller boxes can be used to make a television, washing machine or fridge. Paint these and attach any other parts necessary using scrap materials; for example, use paper-fasteners to attach switches so that they can be turned.

Talk about
How big? What shape? How many?

Outdoor and physical play

Chapter six

As children develop both gross and fine motor skills, they become increasingly aware of their body in space. Physical play provides opportunities for experiencing many maths concepts, especially spatial awareness, speed, time, distance, shape and number.

In stretching up, bending down and turning round, children develop an awareness of space and the associated language. Climbing and throwing high, crawling and creeping low, each present a mathematical experience. See-sawing up and down, walking along and jumping off, squeezing under and lying on top, going in, coming out, sitting in front of or standing behind present spatial experience which can be expressed in words.

Large construction

Objective
Shape and space: building with large shapes.

What you need
A variety of strong, purpose-built construction equipment, including size-related boxes, some with sloping edges, and planks.

What to do
Encourage the children to build their own play apparatus. This gives rise to comparative measurement as they discover that a block is too short or too long for their purposes.

Talk about
What shape? Does it fit? Slope, not enough space, high, not high enough, long, not long enough.

Follow-up
Try making:
- Walls, combining flat surfaces of cubes and cuboids to make walls for 'Humpty Dumpty'. This can be extended into making enclosures for 'houses'.
- A see-saw, by finding the balance point of a plank.
- Bridges which need pillars of equal height.
- A slide which gives experience of a slope or gradient.

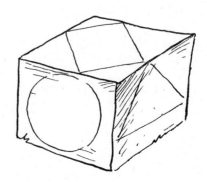

Climbing frames

Objective
Shape and space: talking about position and spatial relationships.

What you need
Equipment such as frames that the children can climb, crawl inside, stand on top of and slide down.

What to do
As the children climb, slide and crawl inside, talk about their position.

Talk about
Where? Inside, on top of, at the side of, high, low, two steps high, between.

Toys with wheels

Objective
Measures: comparing speed using wheels on gradients.

What you need
Wheeled toys and small slopes.

What to do
Encourage the children to push prams, scooters and other wheeled toys up gradual slopes and then down. Safety precautions must be taken to avoid risk to other children.

Talk about
How fast? Slowly, quickly, push, pull, faster than, slower than.

Moving

Objective
Measures: comparing speed and distance using a range of body movements.

What you need
A large floor or grassy area, such as a hall or playing field.

What to do
Play games like 'I can . . .' or variations on 'Simon says . . .'. Ask the children to move in different ways using their body, including walking on tiptoe, with giant strides, hopping, skipping, crawling, rolling and sliding along.

   Children need the chance to run or walk what seems to them 'a long way'. If they are always transported by car they may not have had the experience of running as fast and as far as they are able.

Talk about
How far? How quickly? Fast, slow, a long way, a short distance, faster than, slower than.

Body shapes

Objective
Shape and space: making shapes and using space with the body.

What you need
A large floor or grassed area.

What to do
Ask the children to use their body to make shapes, for example, a flat, thin, round, tall, small or wiggly shape.

   Then ask them to form a line and imitate the action of the leader. This can be made into a 'Pied Piper' game.

Talk about
What shape? Find a space, close together, far apart, in a line, in a row.

Ring games

Objective
Shape and space: making shapes and exploring space using games.

What you need
A large floor or grassed area.

What to do
Ask the children to hold hands and form a circle. Use this for singing traditional ring songs. Adapt 'Here we go round the mulberry bush' to include actions that encourage the children to use space, for example, 'This is the way we jump up high,' or 'turn around' or 'curl up in a ball'.

Talk about
What shape? In a circle, inside, outside.

Follow-up
Hold hands and make arches, sing 'In and out the dusty bluebells'.

Educational visits

Objectives
Investigating shape, space, number, measures and pattern in the environment.

What to do
Consider the possibilities of:
Shape
● The classroom: shape of the clock, water tray, windows, flooring and pipes.
● The outside area: shape of fencing, trees, shed, flower beds, climbing frames and other equipment.
● Local streets: shape of houses, flats, gates, cars, lamp posts and road signs.
● Field trips: for example, at a farm, consider the shape and size of tractor wheels, animals etc; at the seaside, consider the shapes of shells, stones and sails. ·
Pattern
● Look for patterns in roof tiling, brickwork, fabrics, animals' skin, birds' feathers, leaves and flowers.
Measure
● Look for instruments used for measuring — speedometers, weighing machines, theodolites, windsocks, clock towers.
● Compare the sizes of trees, cars, people and animals, and compare the weights of leaves, pebbles and other natural and man-made materials.

Visits and short walks in the locality give children a sense of location and the opportunity to discuss relative distance. Encourage the children to make their own maps of these journeys. Listen as they tell you the features they are including.

Talk about
What shape? What pattern? How far? How heavy? How fast? Near, far, close to, next to, a long way.

Food

Chapter seven

Work in the food area gives rise to the experience of measurement, time, number and pattern. The children can investigate area by covering toast with butter or grated cheese. The use of different-shaped cutters can be explored in making sandwiches and biscuits. The food area enables children to learn about fractions and division as they slice and share food and match one spoonful of mixture to each bun case. Try also tasting and sorting foods into sweet or sour, salt or bitter. These activities need to be supervised.

The food area also provides an opportunity to combine maths with science and health education.

Ask parents for details of any food allergy before starting food activities.

Spreading

Objective
Shape and space: covering an area by spreading margarine over bread.

What you need
Uncut loaf of bread, bread knife, butter or margarine, honey and cheese spread, some blunt knives.

What to do
Use an uncut loaf and slice it for the children. Count how many wish to take part, and estimate how much they can have each. Using the knife, spread margarine over the bread. Offer a choice of honey or cheese spread.

Talk about
Spreading the margarine all over, to the edge.

Follow-up
• Try using different shapes of bread, for example, a French stick or a cob.
• Try using other spreads and toppings, for example, paste, cottage cheese or grated cheese.

Non-standard measures

Objective
Measures: measuring with non-standard measures.

What you need
A simple recipe and ingredients (see *Bright Ideas Early Years Science Activities*, Chapter six).

What to do
Convert standard recipe measurements into non-standard measures using cups and spoons.

Use cups for large amounts of dry or liquid ingredients such as flour or water, and use spoons for small amounts of dry or liquid ingredients such as sugar or milk. It is possible to use spoonfuls of soft margarine.

Talk about
How much? Cupful, tablespoonful, teaspoonful.

Follow-up
Make pictorial recipe cards that feature the cup or spoonfuls that are needed.

Use packet covers or pictures to illustrate the ingredients. Write the words alongside.

Standard measures

Objective
Measures: measuring for weight using standard measures and becoming familiar with the names of standard measures.

What you need
A simple recipe, ingredients, measuring jug and kitchen scales.

What to do
Look together at the recipe. Read aloud the instructions. Encourage the children to participate as fully as possible as you use the jug and scales for measuring. Introduce the terms for measuring dry and liquid ingredients, and emphasise the importance of accuracy.

Talk about
How much? How many? Grams, litres.

Baking

Objectives
Following instructions for a purpose and completing a sequence of related activities.

What you need
Pictorial recipes.

What to do
Using pictorial recipes, ask the children to count and measure the ingredients required. It is more important that the children participate fully in all stages of cooking than that the baking looks perfect.

Talk about
How many? How much?

Cooking

Objective
Measures: introducing time as a meaningful measure.

What to do
While the children wait for the food to bake in the oven or for toast to brown under the grill, discuss how long it will take. Refer to points in the daily routine, for example, 'The bread will be ready at group time'. Refer to standard measures of time, 'In 20 minutes', and refer to the clock. These can be successfully combined to produce a meaningful measure, 'The pie will be ready in ten minutes, at tidy-up time'.

Talk about
How long? Times.

Cutting apples

Objective
Number: understanding fractions by dividing whole objects.

What you need
Apples, knife.

What to do
Decide how many will share each apple. Four is a useful number. Cut the apple in half and then in quarters. Try this using different fruit, such as bananas and oranges. Divide flans and cakes of different shapes equally between a fixed number of children.

Talk about
How much each? The same amount, divide, half, quarter.

Fruit and vegetables

Objective
Number: looking at patterns in nature.

What you need
A fruit or vegetable (try using a cabbage, a kiwi fruit, a lemon or an apple), a knife for adult use. If the children are to cut soft fruits then blunt knives can be provided. This activity needs to be supervised.

What to do
Look closely at the fruit or vegetable. Examine the skin or outside layers. Cut the fruit or vegetable in half. Look at the pattern inside; perhaps there are segments, seeds or layers. Take two fruits; cut one in half lengthways and the other widthways. Compare the patterns.

Talk about
Pattern. What shape? Where? In the middle, on the edge.

Popping corn

Objectives
Shape and space: watching the effect of heat on shape and size, and tasting the difference.

What you need
Popcorn, a transparent saucepan with a lid, vegetable oil.

What to do
Observe the corn, looking at its size, shape, texture and colour.

Warm the oil in the saucepan and add the corn, leaving some corn to compare later. Watch and listen as the corn pops. Take the pan off the heat. Keep the lid on until the popping stops. Spoon out the popcorn and compare it with the original corn.

Talk about
How large? Small, smaller than, bigger than.

Follow-up
Try using other foods that swell on cooking, like rice and pasta. Pasta comes in many interesting shapes, including spirals, tubes, stars, long spaghetti rods and flat sheets of lasagne.

Growing cress

Objectives
Measures: measuring time and recording height changes by growing cress. Looking at covering an area by making cress sandwiches.

What you need
Cress seeds, blotting paper, plastic trays, piece of dark material, scissors.

What to do
Lay the blotting paper in the plastic tray. Sow the seeds on the blotting paper. Cover with a dark piece of material for a few days. Water the seeds regularly, as they dry out rapidly in a warm room. Chart the height as they grow by taking photographs or cutting thread the same length.

Cut the cress using scissors and make cress sandwiches.

Talk about
How high? How long? Two days, yesterday, tomorrow.

Follow-up
Try growing the seeds of fruits tasted in the food area, such as melons, apples and pears.

Shopping list

Objective
Estimating: using maths for everyday activities.

What to do
Invite the children to contribute as you estimate how much food is needed for a planned food activity.

Talk about
How many? How much?

Shopping

Objective
Measures: comparing the weights of everyday items.

What you need
Shopping items – a large packet of cereal, sugar, a tin of syrup and a tin of custard powder.

What to do
Hold up and comment on the weight of each item. Compare items of the same size and compare large, light items such as a packet of breakfast cereal with small, heavy items such as sugar. This is especially important, as children often associate size with weight.

When shopping, take several bags so that the weight can be distributed between the children. They will discover that some bags which are full of light items are easily carried, while others contain only one small item that is difficult to lift.

Talk about
How heavy? Light, heavy, heavier than, lighter than.

Paying for goods

Objectives
Measures: observing how money is used in exchange for goods, and becoming familiar with the names of coins and the language used in financial transactions.

What you need
A shopping list, a shopping bag and money.

What to do
Encourage the children to select the goods required by looking at labels. Present these at the till. A patient assistant at an off-peak time will wait as you and the children sort and count money. Discuss the till with various function keys and the receipt with a date, for recording the transaction. Watch as the assistant looks at the price labels, enters each item, asks for the appropriate sum and sorts the money into compartments.

Talk about
How much does it cost? Change, coin names, price, enough money.

Records

Chapter eight

The children's progress and the curriculum are two areas needing constant evaluation.

The following are several ways of recording children's experiences and activities:
- Taking photographs and drawing plans of models are particularly relevant for recording models made in the construction area.
- Children's paintings, drawing and junk models can be used as records of their activities. Listen as children talk about what they are representing. This may not be immediately obvious to an adult eye, but children's explanations are most revealing.
- Displaying the children's work alongside relevant objects and photographs of visits and activities undertaken, provides an effective means of recording experiences and activities.

You need to be familiar with the attainment targets of the National Curriculum so that you can inform parents, governors and all interested parties how the children are working towards them. On evaluating existing playgroup, nursery and reception class provision and practice, you will discover that the traditional tenets of education for the three- to six-year-olds, namely emphasis on drawing out the mathematical potential of children's play and supporting their acquisition of the relevant language as a base for understanding on shape, space, number and measurement, support the National Curriculum.

Observing and recording children's progress in maths

Invite parents to contribute to their child's records. To do this constructively, they need to be informed about the attitudes, skills and understanding central to a child's development. Provide parent information and a pictorial record sheet, giving a focus for teacher-parent dialogue.

On page 93 is an example of the record sheet used in my nursery, combining both maths and science (see also photocopiable page 96).

The records are pictorial to make them more attractive. They are in the shape of two semi-detached houses, to indicate that the foundations of maths, technology and science are interrelated. They provide a focus for parent information about maths activities at school and home and parents are invited to observe the development of their child and contribute to it. The records give the opportunity for you to discuss a child's achievements with the parents and they are therefore filled in together by you and the parents. To fill in the chart use highlighter pens of appropriate colours to shade sections and date them if required.

What the records show

Attitudes and interest
- Taking part in daily activities at home and at school, the sources of early learning.

- Interest and motivation as indicated by 'chooses' and 'enjoys'.
- Willingness to experiment and explore, which cannot be taken for granted.
- Purposeful play rather than random exploratory play.
- Concentration as children spend longer at activities.
- Thinking ahead and planning as children begin to approach equipment with specific ideas of what they intend to do.

Maths talk

Children's activities give rise to experience that needs to be expressed in words, and maths has its own precise language.
- Use of mathematical language including speed, direction and position.
- The ability to recite number rhymes which are a first step to familiarity with number names.
- Asking questions which demonstrates an interest in looking for answers, pattern and reasons.
- Communicating ideas to others, namely staff and friends.

Mathematical thinking

Observing children's activities shows whether they are willing to:
- Solve problems such as finding a new way of doing something.
- Reason using 'because' and 'if'.
- Classify, describing how things are the same or different.
- Represent, recording their experience in paint, models or movement.
- Predict, guessing what might happen.

Taking part in maths activities

Recording experiences children have taken part in, including:
- Sorting and matching for shape at tidy up time when geometric bricks are replaced on their silhouettes.

- Measuring for height, width, length and weight as part of different activities.
- Using money when shopping with staff or during imaginative play.
- Looking at clocks and watches with staff and using old ones as part of role play.
- Create patterns with bricks and other materials.
- Sorting and matching objects with a common feature and making a collection of objects the same size, shape or colour.

Maths, technology and science

- Enjoys using a computer.
- Enjoys observing and has used a magnifying glass.
- Willing to guess what might happen and test it.
- Willing to talk about what she or he is doing, seeing, hearing, touching, tasting and smelling.
- Has a caring attitude to others and the world.
- Has planted seeds and watched them grow.
- Chooses sand play. Experiments with wet and dry sand.
- Willing to explore and experiment.
- Chooses food area activities.
- Enjoys taking part in school activities.
- Willing to record through modelling, painting, movement etc.
- Can describe parts of the body.
- Enjoys looking after plants, animals and insects.
- Can plan and complete an activity.
- Chooses water play. Experiments e.g. floating, sinking, displacement etc.
- Asks questions especially why?
- Enjoys using clay and dough.
- Willing to work with others.
- Repeats activity to see if it happens again.
- Concentrates on chosen activity.
- Enjoys taking part in household activities.
- Chooses to sort and match objects with a common feature.
- Knows a number rhyme (e.g. Once I caught a fish alive).
- Represents in models, paint etc.
- Enjoys role play.
- Chooses construction. Make towers, walls and houses. Makes appropriate use of wheels.
- Uses the word 'because' and reasons why.
- Can relate photos and pictures to real objects.
- Enjoys fitting things together and taking them apart.
- Has experienced measuring for height, weight and length.
- Knows that clocks are used to mark time.
- Enjoys physical play, climbing, balancing, running, hopping and wheeled toys.
- Can replace equipment and geometric blocks on to their silhouettes.
- Enjoys problem solving.
- Makes patterns with bricks, beads boxes etc.
- Knows that money is used when shopping.
- Describes how things are different.
- Chooses junk modelling and uses materials of a variety of shape, size and texture.
- Describes how things are the same.
- Talks about direction e.g. from, out of, into, to.
- Talks about speed e.g. fast, slow.
- Talks about position e.g. on top, over, under, behind.
- Willing to tidy up and replace objects where they belong.

Designed by Caroline Matusiak

Book list

Staff library

Sand and Water, ILEA Learning Materials Service (E J Arnold).

Structuring Play in the Early Years at School, Kathleen Manning and Ann Sharp (Ward Lock Educational).

Early Mathematical Experiences, Schools Council (Addison-Wesley).

Parent library

Maths Through Play, Rose Griffiths (Macdonald).

Ready for Maths, Chris Heald and Val Eustice (Hippo).

Parents' Guide to Your Child's Maths, Ruth Merttens (The Parent and Child Programme Octopus).

Resources

General
Clock
Height chart
Day, date and weatherboard
Jigsaws and table games
Pattern boards eg mosaics
Computer toy

Construction
A set of large, strong construction equipment including boxes and planks
A set of size related bricks offering a variety of shapes
Construction materials eg LEGO, Duplo, Mobilo and Sticklebricks
Scrap materials including wood
Railway and roadway
Rulers of different lengths including metre measure
Clipboard with pencil attached for making plans

Dry sand and water
Funnels, jugs and bottles in three sizes based on a litre
Spoons — teaspoon, tablespoon and ladle
An assortment of irregular bottles and containers
Colander and sieve
Sand or waterwheel
Plastic tubing
Small figures, vehicles and animals

Wet sand and dough
Rolling pins or cylinders of different

diameter
Patterned surfaces for printing eg potato
masher and combs
Moulds, plastic scrap materials
Cutters including tools eg wooden splice
Containers of different shapes and sizes
Balance and bucket scales

Paint

Objects for printing including bricks,
boxes and an assortment of irregular
shapes eg leaves and string
Brushes of different thickness including
fine and decorating brushes
Safety mirror

Role play

Dolls in two or three sizes with fitting
clothes
Clocks and watches, play or old ones
Money real or pretend
Teacher-made cheque books and bank
cards
Till, purse and shopping bag

Order forms and catalogues
A set of tableware and cutlery
Pans in three sizes with fitting lids

Story

Puppets
Felt board and figures
Story books including:
'Goldilocks and the Three Bears'
'The Three Little Pigs'
The Very Hungry Caterpillar, Eric Carle
(Picture Puffin)
Titch, Pat Hutchins (Picture Puffin)
There's No Such Thing as a Dragon, Jack
Kent (Blackie)
Shapes of Things, Althea (Dinosaur)
This Little Puffin, E Matterson (Penguin)

Food area

Baking equipment
Standard measures like teaspoon and
litre jug
Non-standard measures like cups
Scales

Maths, technology and science

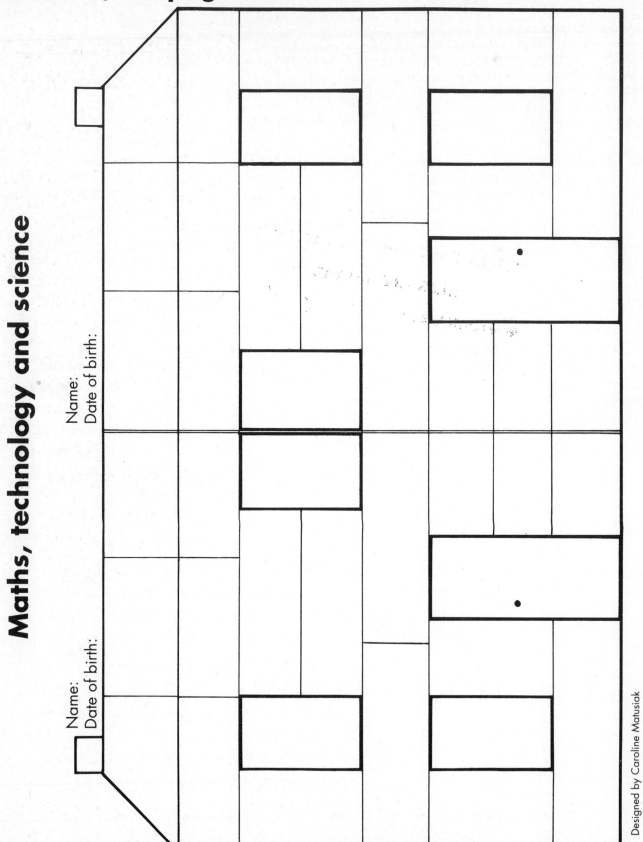

Name:
Date of birth:

Name:
Date of birth:

Designed by Caroline Matusiak